PROLOGUE

It is a hot, humid afternoon in New York City. The date: July 2, 1982. On lower Fifth Avenue, people stroll by in shorts and T-shirts, fanning themselves. For them, it is just another ordinary summer day.

But for a small group of people standing clustered around the stage of the Peppermint Lounge nightclub on Fifth Avenue near 15th Street, there is nothing ordinary about the day at all. Simon Le Bon, Nick Rhodes, John Taylor, Andy Taylor, and Roger Taylor (collectively known as Duran Duran) are on that stage, and they are soundchecking in preparation for their performance that night.

"Ready to go!" the sound engineer calls out, and the band launches into the sound that is its trademark. Orange-haired Nick Rhodes, wearing a black leather jacket and looking like a mischievous leprechaun, attacks his banks of keyboards and produces an ethereal sound; Roger Taylor and John Taylor, dark heads nodding in unison, provide a fluid rhythm; and Andy Taylor brings in the swirling chords of his guitar to create a wall of sound that stuns everyone in the room.

Then Simon Le Bon steps up to the microphone, pushing a lock of dark-blond hair off his forehead. He brings one shoulder up slightly and tilts the microphone stand forward as he sings.

It is a very special moment. The few people gathered around on the floor stand with their mouths open as the band joins in with "girls on film, girls on film." John is

7

These guys really get a lot of enjoyment out of playing.

excited as he swings his bass guitar from side to side, his lanky frame following, and there is a smile on Andy's expressive face as he plays.

What the people in that nightclub are witnessing is something very, very special. It is one of the last times Duran Duran will play in a club in the United States. It will be a superb performance that will leave a tightly-packed club roaring for more after three encores. The group's newest album, *Rio*, will become the hottest album in the country within a few months. The night before the Peppermint Lounge date, the group had sold out an 8000-seat outdoor concert on Manhattan's Pier 44. In a few days, the group would open for Blondie at New Jersey's Meadowlands to wilder acclaim than the headliner. This is a band poised on the brink of unbelievable success, and everyone at the Peppermint Lounge can sense it.

I was fortunate enough to be there that night, and although I had followed the band since the beginning, I was mesmerized by what I heard and saw: magic, right there in front of me. From that day, I have been a Duran Duran fan. I have also been lucky enough to spend time with Simon, Nick, John, Andy, and Roger, and those times are some of my most treasured memories.

I hope that in this book I can help you appreciate Duran Duran as I do. People sometimes say that the members of Duran Duran are empty pretty-boys, that their music lacks greatness, that they simply turn out mindless dance music for mindless listeners.

I disagree. Duran Duran—besides being five of the nicest people I have ever met—is the sound and the look of music today. In fact, to borrow a famous advertising slogan: Duran Duran is *it*!

If you don't already feel this way, I hope this book will convince you. Enjoy it!

ONE BY ONE

ONE BY ONE

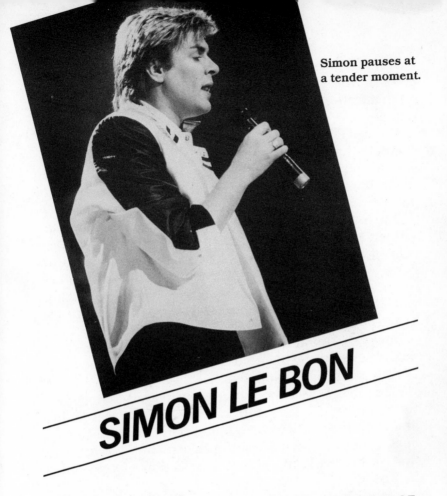

Simon pauses at
a tender moment.

SIMON LE BON

Simon John Charles Le Bon was born on October 27, 1958, at Bushey Maternity Hospital, which is near Watford, England. His astrological sign is Scorpio.

Simon is the eldest of three sons (his brothers are David and Jonathon). His family is descended from the Huguenots—French Protestants who escaped from Catholic France in the sixteenth and seventeenth centuries when they were persecuted by the government of the time. The family originally came from the Normandy area of France. The family's coat of arms can be found on the Huguenot crypt in Canterbury Cathedral.

13

Simon enjoys having an unusual name (it means "the good" in French). His fellow members of Duran Duran often affectionately call him "Charley," using his middle name.

Simon's father is an executive with the National Water Council division of the British civil service. His mother was an actress before her marriage and now runs a hotel in Florida. Simon terms his family "totally middle class," adding that "it's a very secure kind of background."

One of Simon's earliest memories of his childhood in Pinner, Middlesex, near London, is of being in a stroller "and going over this hard, pebbly concrete road and going 'aaa-aaa-aaa-aaa' as it would sound all shaky because of the hard wheels." This early talent for singing was not lost upon his mother, who began sending him to acting classes at the age of five.

However, Simon insists, "I wasn't forced to go to stage school or anything like that. I just did the work because I had a pretty face, I suppose."

When Simon was about ten, Mr. Turvey, the choirmaster at Pinner Parish Church, noticed his vocal ability and got him to sing treble (soprano) in the choir. He was one of the choir's outstanding soloists and cut his very first record with the choir, a collection of traditional hymns.

Despite his success in the choir, Simon continued his acting studies. He began to appear in stage productions in London, including a West End (the equivalent of New York's Broadway) staging of *Tom Brown's Schooldays*. He also starred in TV commercials for a detergent called Persil, for a magazine called *Look In*, and (as his fellow music superstar Michael Jackson would later do) for Pepsi!

Simon's creative fashion sense was also beginning to show itself, in an amusing way. He recalls now, "The first time I became fashion-conscious was when I realized I was the only boy left at my school still wearing short trousers."

Simon compares musical notes with the Rolling Stones' Ron Wood.

School is a sore subject for Simon. Though it may not seem very likely now, he was not very popular with girls at that time. He didn't even have a girlfriend until age sixteen. Also, although his teachers remember him as highly intelligent, he was never particularly interested in academic topics. When it came time for the A levels (tests that every student in England planning to go on to a university must take), he flunked all but one of them.

After that, Simon did a number of things. He went to art school for a term; he became an apprentice to a printer for a short time; he went to Israel on a holiday and worked on a kibbutz; and he even worked as a tree surgeon for a while.

While he was in art school in 1977, he founded his first band, a punk group called Dog Days. The group only played publicly once, at a dance at a school called Harrow Tech, but Simon remembers it fondly.

"It was great!" he grins. "We were bottom of the bill underneath Supercharge, a band called 98th Precinct, and some other art school band. We got turned off because we went on for too long. They pulled my mike

"I like to write things which I don't completely understand myself," Simon admits to the press.

out and I went over to somebody else's—it was really funny!"

With this sort of success smiling at the group, Dog Days soon disbanded, and Simon decided it was time to go back to school. He got a job as a porter in a hospital and went to night school to earn another A level.

Upon completion of his night course, Simon applied to Birmingham University for a drama course and was accepted. Soon after that he met and joined up with Duran Duran. (You'll find *that* story later on.)

Simon is considered Duran Duran's poet, and he writes all of the group's lyrics. They are sometimes difficult to comprehend, although Simon admits, "I like to write things which I don't completely understand myself."

Until recently, Simon lived with his father and brother David in the family home in Middlesex. However, his recent engagement to a Canadian model, Claire Stansfield, changed that. They now share an apartment in Toronto and a house in London, and Claire accompanies him on most tours.

"We're the happiest couple in the whole wide world," Simon insists. "But we don't know yet when we're getting married."

Doubtless Simon's marriage will disappoint many of his fans—he describes the letters he receives from them as "very romantic." Many of his admirers, though, say that they are very pleased for him and wish him every happiness.

Asked for a self-portrait, Simon responded this way: "Eastern jangles, flashes, jungles, all purple, gold and red, a crimson flag to herald the dawn and from the center of the liquid flame steps the man."

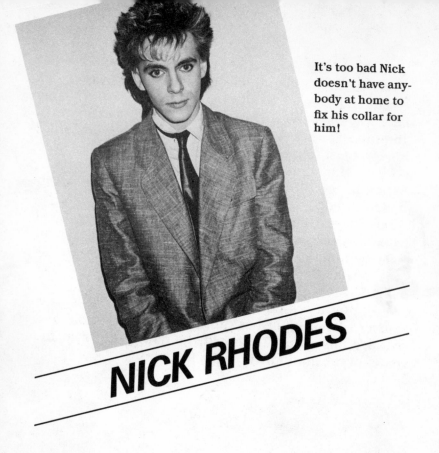

It's too bad Nick doesn't have anybody at home to fix his collar for him!

NICK RHODES

Nicholas James Bates (he changed his name to Rhodes) was born in Birmingham, England. His father is an engineer, and he describes his mother as a "happy housewife."

"I'm a Gemini," Nick says, "and I believe in immense detail." He also admits to an intense curiosity about the world, and, in fact, his very first memory is of mixing stones in with his mother's potatoes to see what her reaction would be.

His curiosity, however, did not show itself much in school, which he hated. "School really stifled me," he says. "I really didn't feel that I needed to know what sodium bicarbonate and sulfuric acid make."

But one thing positive did come out of formal education for Nick. "The main thing I learned at school," he muses, "which was invaluable to me later on, was about people and psychology."

Another thing he learned to do, perhaps because of his lack of interest in classes, was to fantasize about the future. "I wanted to be a pop star since I was about twelve," he reminisces. "But then, of course, it's a dream." Nonetheless, he asserts, "I had a very vivid impression of what I wanted to do."

What he wanted to do was leave school and play music, which he did as soon as he turned sixteen and passed his O levels (tests required for a diploma), although he says now, "I swore when I left school that I was never going to use any of my O levels or anything, ever. I knew they were entirely useless to me."

A rare smile from Nick during a performance.

Of all the Durans, Nick seems to prefer suits the most.

What was useful to him was a passionate interest in music, especially in artists such as David Bowie, Bryan Ferry of Roxy Music, and Rod Stewart. Not coincidentally, he was also very interested in clothes and in hanging out at Birmingham nightclubs such as Barbarella's.

All of this led to his getting together with his childhood friend John Taylor (who had grown up down the block from him) to form a band that would embrace all of their interests. (More about that later.)

Nick is very fond of animals, especially cats, and says sadly that what upsets him the most is "animals dying," although he is not a vegetarian because "I like steak too much, unfortunately!"

Does he have any pets of his own? "I did have some pets when I used to live at home with my parents a few years back, and they're still there. My mum has to look after them because I travel so much and I can't look after them. I've got a black cat called Sebastian and a black-and-white collie dog called Raffles." He laughingly adds that "the cat gets more fan mail than me!"

Nick also enjoys French food, strawberries, champagne, all kinds of films (especially those starring Marilyn Monroe, Elizabeth Taylor, and Sophia Loren), "Family Feud" (one of his favorite phrases is "good answer, good answer"), and sleeping.

New places he'd like to go to include China, Iceland, Russia, and Brazil. He says that his current favorite cities are "London, New York and Paris—not necessarily in that order!" He has a house in a chic section of London.

Orange-haired Nick—his hair has been fifteen different colors at different times—talks in a very animated way, using his hands to emphasize a point. His green eyes flash when he speaks.

Although he is known as the comedian of the group and does joke around a lot, he can be very serious.

Nick is often chosen as the band's spokesman because he has such a thoughtful way of expressing himself.

John is quite outspoken, and his views are sometimes controversial.

JOHN TAYLOR

John was born Nigel John Taylor on June 20, 1960, in Birmingham, England. He later switched his name around because he liked the way it sounded. Photos of him as a baby show someone already tall for his age, with an angelic smile and a wicked gleam in his eye.

Dark-haired, dark-eyed John is an only child. His father is a white-collar worker at a car-parts factory. His mother works part-time in a school cafeteria. They still live in the same house in the Birmingham suburb of Hollywood that John was raised in.

Like the other members of the band, John showed little interest in school, preferring to listen to David

Bowie records with his friends and read the English music paper, the *New Musical Express*. One bright spot for John was his discovery that music lessons were given at school. But when he asked the teacher for guitar lessons, he was informed that only "proper orchestra instruments" were taught. Soon after that, he got his first guitar and taught himself to play. He later switched to bass when he became fascinated with funk.

John now says that he wishes he'd learned to play the piano and paid more attention in language classes, but he still recalls, "I'd be sitting there and I'd think, 'Well, what's the point of this? I wish they'd teach me to drive instead.' "

He next went on to art college. At first, he did very well, earning top grades for his first project. "I did the whole thing on black plastic," he says, "and only used red,

Johns gets very excited when he plays live.

John says he'd really like to stop smoking.

black, and white, 'cause I was on a red, black, and white trip at the time."

He was not as fortunate the next time, though, when he attempted to make his final presentation of the year the first Duran Duran demo tape. "They didn't quite know how to handle it," he grins, "but they had to give me the benefit of the doubt and pass me for the course."

John, who still lives in Birmingham, is a James Bond fanatic who owns video copies of all the Bond movies, though the ones starring Sean Connery (especially *Goldfinger*) are his favorites. He confesses that he is hooked on Bond "to the point of obsession."

His obsession with Bond even affects his other obsession, cars—he recently bought a Bond-type gold Aston Martin. He also loves Porsches, BMWs, and any kind of Mercedes-Benz.

John loves to go out to nightclubs and parties in whatever city he happens to be in, and describes himself as "a pretty cheerful sort of chap."

He also has a secret fondness for Big Macs.

Andy ponders the meaning of life.

ANDY TAYLOR

Andrew Taylor was born at Tynemouth Royal Infirmary, near Newcastle, England, on February 16, 1961. He is an Aquarius, but is too practical to believe in astrology.

Andy's father was a fisherman and so was his grandfather, and he grew up in the tiny coastal village of Cullercoats. His family was very poor, and Andy spent his early years using an outside toilet and washing up in a tin bath.

Early in his school career, Andy did well enough to be accepted into an academically superior "grammar

Music is the most important thing in Andy's life. "When your heart's in something, you just do it," he says.

school" (prep school) at age eleven. But his happiness at his new school was to be short-lived.

"The first day I went to grammar school," he recalls, "—dead exciting, you know—well, I came home and my mother had gone! So I thought, Oh, well, it's just me and my old man and my little brother. . . . "

Soon after this, the family moved to nearby Whitley Bay, and Andy transferred to a lower-ranked comprehensive school, in which he quickly lost interest. His father, because of a decline in the fishing industry, had been forced to become a carpenter. Hoping that his son would avoid a similar fate, he encouraged the young Andy to continue practicing the guitar he had taken up at the age of five.

That suited Andy fine. He put together a band and played his first professional gig when he was just thirteen.

"I totally lost interest in school," he recalls, "became a real bum and drop-out, never used to go at all. And then I became the black-sheep kid at school 'cause I had long hair and played in groups, and all the rest of the lads were going camping or something. . . . I wasn't into that."

Andy was into playing, and he devoted himself to that. Teachers tried to help him by educating him in a trade such as bricklaying or plumbing, but he was just not interested.

"I got into all sorts of trouble at school," he says. "But when your heart's in something, you just do it. I didn't even think about it really."

Eventually he just stopped attending class altogether, and started playing all the time with various bands, first at local bars in the north of England, and later at clubs and military bases in Europe.

Andy had the experience of spending time playing with several different groups (often changing groups every few months) in many unusual places. He played for ten weeks at a Greek beach club; he also played a thirteen-month stint in Germany, just as one of his favorite groups, the Beatles, did early on in their career.

Andy also had a frightening experience in Luxembourg. His band was owed almost $4000 by a club owner there, and when he went to ask for the money, he was held at gunpoint by local police.

However, this did not dampen Andy's enthusiasm for music, and upon his return home from one of his European trips, he saw an ad in the paper that would lead him directly to Duran Duran.

Andy is appreciated by the rest of the band for his dry sense of humor and his ability with figures. He is the only Duran who actually likes business meetings.

His main dislike is for "arty-farty conversations." He also dislikes pretense, aggravation, and "losing my temper."

Andy changed his name to Andrew Wilson-Taylor upon his marriage to hairstylist Tracey Wilson in August 1982. Rather than cancel the band's American tour that summer, Andy flew Tracey out to Los Angeles and they had a formal wedding at the Chateau Marmont there.

Although Andy used to be known as someone who worked hard and played hard, since his marriage he has calmed down a lot. He and Tracey have settled into a comfortable house in Wolverhampton. They also own a loft in London, a restaurant called Rio in Newcastle, and a fifteenth-century cottage in Shropshire, with enough land to raise animals.

In fact, animals are now an important part of Andy's life, and he helps run a charity home for them. However, he also says that one of his pet peeves is "dogs messing on the carpet."

Roger is always so dapper. People often compare him to James Dean.

ROGER TAYLOR

Roger Andrew Taylor was born on April 26, 1960, in Castle Bromwich, near Birmingham. He is a typical Taurus in that he is very stubborn, but quite shy.

Roger's father worked in the automobile industry, like many of the men in Birmingham. "It was either that or escape," dark-haired, dark-eyed Roger says. "You could either escape through football or music. And I wasn't much good at football."

"I've always been the quiet one," Roger admits.

His talent for music became evident at age ten, when he began to bang on pots with knitting needles. Soon after that, he went to see his first concert—featuring the Jackson Five. This might partly have been because of his older brother, who was a big Motown fan.

However, Roger's taste in music soon ran to punk. He joined up with a series of Birmingham bands that have since been described as "eminently forgettable." The only two that are remembered, probably because of their strange names, are Crucified Toad and the Scent Organs. It was when he was playing with the latter group that Roger was approached at a party and asked to audition for Duran Duran.

Roger is the shiest member of the group and hates being interviewed. "I've always been the quiet one," he confesses. "The kid who sat at the back of the class and said nothing. I'm not a natural extrovert and I have to admit that the fans get on top of me at times."

His favorite era is the '50s. He loves movies of that period, and his favorite actors are Montgomery Clift, Marlon Brando, and Tony Curtis. In fact, he has been described as having a Tony Curtis haircut, and people often say that he is a James Dean lookalike.

He enjoys the music of Peter Gabriel, fellow drummer Phil Collins, and Genesis. Roger says that his idea of a good time is to lie in bed and watch TV.

Roger still lives at home with his parents (because being away from his family makes him sad), but he is looking for a place in London. He tries to bring a bit of home with him wherever he goes by taking records and tapes.

Roger likes dogs and hates cats, and always wears white socks.

THE FAB FIVE

THE FAB FIVE

"What do you mean?" John, Simon, and Nick seem to be asking.

THE SOUND OF THUNDER: The Beginning

It was the summer of 1978. John Taylor, then in art school, got together with his childhood friend Nick Rhodes to try to form a band. At the time, the punk movement was overtaking England, and they felt that they wanted to bring a more elegant sound to music.

In those days, John was still playing guitar and Nick had a WASP synthesizer (which was the least expensive kind that could be bought at the time) and an electronic rhythm unit. They then recruited two local musicians: Steve Duffy on vocals and bass and Simon Colley on bass and clarinet.

They rehearsed for a while, and soon had a few songs worked out. People who heard them play then report that their sound was very obviously influenced by David Bowie. Soon this early group managed to get a booking at Barbarella's, which was Birmingham's hippest club at the time, supporting a local band called Fashion.

Now they had their first date to play and no name. Nick remembers exactly how they coined one.

"John and I were having a lunchtime drink in the Hole in the Wall (a pub in Birmingham), trying to decide [on] a name. We'd been through everything. We'd been through books, film titles, we'd looked on walls and in the dictionary. We'd made up words and everything a band usually does. There is one name I remember— RAF. It didn't stand for anything, we just liked it.

"Then the film *Barbarella* came up in conversation, and I think it was John who said, 'Duran Duran, that doesn't sound bad! What about that for a name?' And there it was."

(Just in case you're not familiar with *Barbarella*, it was a 1960s science-fiction spoof that starred Jane Fonda and featured the character actor Milo O'Shea as Duran Duran, a weird angel.)

The name stuck, but the original members didn't. Simon Colley quit first after only a few weeks, because he wanted to play in a more straight-ahead rock 'n' roll band. Steve Duffy left soon afterward, saying that he wanted to write a novel called *Wednesday Jones* about the problems of growing up in Birmingham. (That novel has never been published, but Steve put out a single in England in 1983 under the name "Tin Tin.")

Nick and John didn't let these defections stop them. They asked Andy Wickett, who up until then was singing with one of their favorite Birmingham bands, TV Eye, to join them. He did.

It was at about this time that one of Duran Duran's best-known songs came into being. Either John or Nick ("We'll argue about it until the cows come home, so there's no point," grins John) came up with the chorus to "Girls on Film," which has survived to this day.

Another change in the band's lineup was about to happen. "My rhythm unit only had rhumba, foxtrot, slow rock, fast rock, and swing on it," Nick explains cheerfully, "so we decided that we needed a drummer to compensate.

"Andy Wickett was out one night at a party and approached this James Dean lookalike, Roger Taylor, who was once a member of the hideously titled Birmingham combo Crucified Toad, but was currently playing in the semilegendary Scent Organs. Fortunately, Andy had noticed the young lad's skin-bashing potential and had the cheek to invite our Rodge down to a rehearsal. The next day . . . no, *that* day, he joined. And things have been downhill ever since!" Nick concludes with a laugh.

John recalls that Roger could "hit as many drums as possible in a tenth of a second. He was the only one in Birmingham who could keep up with Nick's WASP going 'deet-deet-deet-deet-deet-deet-deet tzunda tzunda tzunda dada dada'!"

These skills firmly in place, Roger, Andy Wickett, Nick, and John got together to make the very first Duran Duran demo tape with Birmingham producer Bob Lamb, best known for his work with the reggae band UB40.

On this tape, John played both guitar and bass, but he was about to switch to bass only. Part of the reason

John, Simon, and Nick have always listened carefully to each other's ideas.

for this, John says, was that in listening to records by the disco group Chic, "that was the first time that I actually realized that the bass player really does guide the tune."

Also, John explains, "there was the excitement of hearing Roger play. We'd never had a drummer before and I really wanted to play with him so I was going half and half. We'd say, well, let's try this one number and play bass with him and then we'd play another number—this is in rehearsals—playing guitar. And I just settled in. I felt so comfortable playing with Rodge, it was just a natural decision, really."

That decision, however, left the band without a guitarist, and so an ad was placed in the paper for a "modern guitarist for Roxy/Bowie-influenced band." Soon Londoner Alan Curtis joined, as did singer Jeff Thomas, who was previously with Roger's old band, the Scent Organs.

With this lineup, they were ready to look for places to play again. One day Nick and John took the band's demo tape into a new Birmingham club called the Rum Runner, which was already the new "in" place in town. It was one of their favorite places to go because they could hear all the music they liked there: David Bowie, Roxy Music, and Chic.

The owners of the club, Paul and Michael Berrow, were very impressed with Duran Duran. They not only offered the band gigs, but also a place to rehearse. (Up until then, the band had been playing in an abandoned building in the industrial section of town.) Eventually, the Berrow brothers also began to manage the band, which they still do to this day.

Despite the fact that things seemed to be looking good, Alan Curtis and Jeff Thomas soon left the band. In the next few months, Nick, John, and Roger auditioned dozens and dozens of singers and guitarists. Some even became members of the band for brief periods of time.

But the guys weren't happy. They had an exact idea of what they wanted, but they didn't seem to be getting it. Finally, they decided to place an ad in a national music newspaper, *Melody Maker*. One of the people who responded was Andy Taylor.

"They were the biggest bunch of weirdos that I'd ever seen," Andy recalls. Nonetheless, they all got along well, though, Andy says, "Nick didn't like me because I had jeans on." That didn't seem to matter much, because "John just thought I was the best guitar player that he'd ever seen and played with. Fitting into a band takes time, but the spirit was right and it was just what I wanted to do."

Nick remembers it a little bit differently as he says jokingly of Andy, "He was such a noisy sod and he had such a big mouth and pushed things so much that he threatened us we'd fall apart if he didn't join. So he pressurized us into allowing him to play guitar."

But there was something that they had conveniently forgotten to tell Andy. That was that they had no singer. "So when he arrived at the first rehearsal," Nick laughs, "he said, 'Well, where's the singer?' 'Oh, he's not here today, he's on holiday. But we're gonna try some new ones out.' "

One of the new ones they had in mind was a guy whom Fiona Kemp, a barmaid at the Rum Runner, had dated. His name was Simon Le Bon, and his first appearance made quite an impression upon Nick and Roger.

"This chap turned up in pink leopard-skin trousers, brown suede jacket, dark glasses, and pointed boots," Nick reminisces. "He said his name was Le Bon, and I thought, *No!* He can't be called *Le Bon*."

Nick also remembers thinking. "Anyone who looks that stupid is positively the one."

Roger echoes that thought, saying, "We knew instantly that he was the one."

Simon continues the story. "We seemed to get on very well actually, and they said, 'Come along tomorrow night, all the rest of the band will be here and we'll play a few numbers then.' "

Simon went home, wrote some lyrics he called "The Sound of Thunder" (the same song that appears on the first album), and went back the next night.

At that rehearsal, Simon sang those lyrics to a tune the band had been working on, and something special happened.

"It was one of those magic moments," John says. "We were all playing and we looked around at each other and said, 'Yeah, this is it.' "

After a few weeks of rehearsing, the final lineup of Duran Duran made its debut at the Edinburgh Festival. For Simon, it was a turning point.

"Right, that's it," he remembers deciding, "I'm going to drop out of university."

The other Durans also quit their day jobs at around the same time (Roger worked in a factory, John and Andy did odd jobs at the Rum Runner, and Nick was a deejay). With that, every member of the band was committed to success, as were the Berrow brothers, who invested in the band by buying the members new instruments.

It was also at this time that Duran Duran made the sensible (but, among bands, unusual) decision to split all profits five ways, helping to avoid the financial disagreements and tensions that affect so many groups.

The group was not quite as fortunate with record companies. "We had two main ones lined up and they were a bit sort of, you know, 'There's lots of bands around at the moment, you have to try a bit harder, do a few more live shows, make another demo . . .' " Simon says sarcastically.

The band opted for more live experience. "If you rehearse nine days a week, you become very good rehears-

Poised at the brink of success, John, Roger, Simon, Andy, and Nick contemplate a frilly future.

ing," Nick remembers the brilliant session guitarist Chris Spedding saying to him. "If you play nine dates a week, you become very good at playing live."

Duran Duran learned lessons about playing live by going on the road supporting Hazel O'Connor, who was very popular in Britain at the time, in November of 1980.

Although Michael Berrow had to sell his house to raise the cash the band needed to go on tour, and the guys wound up sleeping in their equipment van and earning about $20 a week each, it was an invaluable experience for Duran Duran.

"It did us so much good," says John. "It meant we played everywhere from Manchester Apollo to the Marquee, tested them out, and learned how to win an audience."

They also won over a record company, and by the end of the tour were committed to sign a worldwide recording deal with EMI Records (Capitol Records, their U.S. label, is a branch of that company). The contract gave them their own Tritec label and what then seemed to them the vast sum of $100 a week each.

Now they were truly on their way to the top.

THIS IS PLANET EARTH: The First Album

In February 1981, Duran Duran released their first single, "Planet Earth." At the time, Nick described their music as "somewhere between the Monkees and Kraftwerk," although he would later call it "a cross between the Sex Pistols and Chic." Whatever it was, people loved it, and the single reached No. 12 on the British charts, which is very good for a debut.

Unfortunately, it was at about this time that the British music press, which is well known for disliking anything popular, decided that Duran Duran "celebrate superficiality," as the *New Musical Express* sneered.

Perhaps part of the reason the members of the press felt this way was that Simon, Nick, John, Andy, and Roger were going through a phase at the time. They were dressing up in the then-popular New Romantic style of frilly clothes and lots of makeup, which groups such as Visage and the early Spandau Ballet also did.

Nick admits that they did that for a reason. "I think the image was obviously very important to us, after the music," he says.

Simon puts it a bit more bluntly. "We jumped on the bandwagon," he says dryly. "We got our feet in the door as quick as we . . . could. We needed something to give the band a sort of personality—and it worked!"

It's the best foot forward as the group meets the press.

But it is John who best sums up the contradictions of that time. "Looking back, it was a good thing because it gave us our own headspace. Nobody's ever really known what to make of us. They never really knew whether we were five Polaroids EMI had got together or whether we were the new Queen."

In the video for "Planet Earth" and in early photographs, they are seen in heavy eye makeup, wearing ruffled shirts, and swathed in scarves and sashes. Nick and Andy both sport platinum-blond hair, cut in a helmet-like shape, while Simon's hair is dyed black and artistically tousled, reminding the viewer of Heathcliff in the classic film *Wuthering Heights.*

But all that was soon to change. As Simon puts it, "After a month or two, we just had to get out of the New Romantic thing, because the frilly shirts looked really stupid!"

After a fling with tailored suits and the semimilitary look, the guys decided to relax. Sighs Nick with obvious relief, "Since we realized that we didn't all have to wear things that didn't suit us and try to be something that we weren't, I think the image has improved greatly. And now it's really just five individuals."

John adds, "Now we have nothing to be frightened of and nothing to hide."

Their first album, titled *Duran Duran,* was released in both England and America in June 1981. It contained "Planet Earth" and two other single hits, "Careless Memories" and "Girls on Film."

"Careless Memories," with its pounding beat, became a huge dance-floor hit on both sides of the Atlantic. "Girls on Film" had a more interesting fate: It became notorious.

The reason such a fuss was made over the song was simple: video. The "Girls on Film" video was too strong for some people's tastes. In fact, the video was banned by England's BBC and only permitted on MTV after severe editing. But in nightclubs and private homes everywhere, people were watching the video.

That video made people take notice of Duran Duran as video artists. Says Nick of the group's ability, "We view videos more as an art form; rather than banging out a promotional video, we try to put them together as we put our records together."

This ability helped the group become wildly popular in England. All three singles from the first album sold extremely well, and by the end of the year the now-familiar sight of girls screaming and fainting at Duran Duran concerts had become commonplace.

And there were frequent Duran Duran concerts, culminating in a triumphant, whirlwind tour of England. This tour included two nights at London's prestigious Hammersmith Odeon and a very special return home—three nights at the Birmingham Odeon.

Despite the group's success in England, and two quick trips to America, Duran Duran was not achieving quite as much success in the United States. But that, too, would soon change.

HUNGRY LIKE THE WOLF:
The Second Album

The beginning of 1982 found the members of Duran Duran back in the recording studio, concentrating on the making of their second album, *Rio*. It was not always an easy time.

John recalls, "We found our identity in such a short space of time. *Rio* is probably the first *real* Duran Duran album, because it's *honestly* us, and it's us playing off each other.

"We'd gone through a lot of personality conflicts when we were doing *Rio* because we were all growing up so much," he continues, "so it was quite difficult 'cause we were niggling with each other and taking sides. But then when it was made we all sat there and we thought, 'Well, we can argue all we like but musically it just hangs together perfectly.' And then we said, 'Well, what are we arguing about?' "

Happy with the finished product, the members of the band found their next stop Sri Lanka, where they were to do the "Hungry like the Wolf," "Save a Prayer," and "Lonely in Your Nightmare" videos.

(Sri Lanka is an island at the tip of the Indian subcontinent and is sometimes called by its old name of Ceylon.)

Nick explains how they came to choose that exotic location. "Our manager went there on holiday, and we were asking him one day, just by coincidence, where there were temples and jungle, and whatever else—we were describing things we wanted to encompass within the videos—and he said, 'I went to Sri Lanka not long ago—we should go there.'"

It turned out to be a fortunate decision on all their parts because, as you know by now, the videos turned out beautifully. (Nick says modestly, "It worked out very well!")

The next stop was Australia, where they had already had a No. 1 single with "Planet Earth," and they were received enthusiastically.

It was at the end of that tour that Andy collapsed on stage from a combination of exhaustion and an intestinal virus he had picked up in Sri Lanka. He recovered in time for the group to tour Japan, where they were

"Why-y-y don't you use it?" Simon yelps during "The Reflex."

47

followed by crowds of girls wherever they went. One afternoon police even had to close down a store that they were shopping in because a riot was about to start!

"Everyone just becomes people, it's great! Music is the only international language in the world!" Andy says happily of the band's world travels.

They were soon to put that international language to the test in an English-speaking country—the U.S.A.! First, though, they made a stop in Antigua, an island in the Caribbean, to make two more videos: "Rio" and "Night Boat." Then it was on to America.

America is traditionally a hard market to crack for bands that are not already well known. Because it is such a large country, tours are very expensive to mount. Also, radio stations are scattered throughout the country (in England, they are national), and so it is difficult to get lots of people interested in a new record at the same time.

But the members of Duran Duran were determined. They played for audiences all over the country, ranging in size from 600 to 40,000. They opened a number of dates for Blondie, on what would turn out to be that pop/new-wave group's final tour.

They played, and played well, nearly every night. But the album was still not doing very well on the U.S. charts, and the band was beginning to get discouraged.

"We were halfway through the tour, losing twenty pounds a day," John recalls, "and we said, 'If the album dies, we're going home.' "

"We had almost lost hope," Roger assents. "To be honest, I couldn't see *Rio* being a big record in America."

But Capitol, the band's U.S. label, was hoping to prove Roger wrong. In July, Capitol released *Carnival*, a four-song mini-album which featured extended dance versions and a more rocking, more aggressive sound. Soon, the band began to get more radio play.

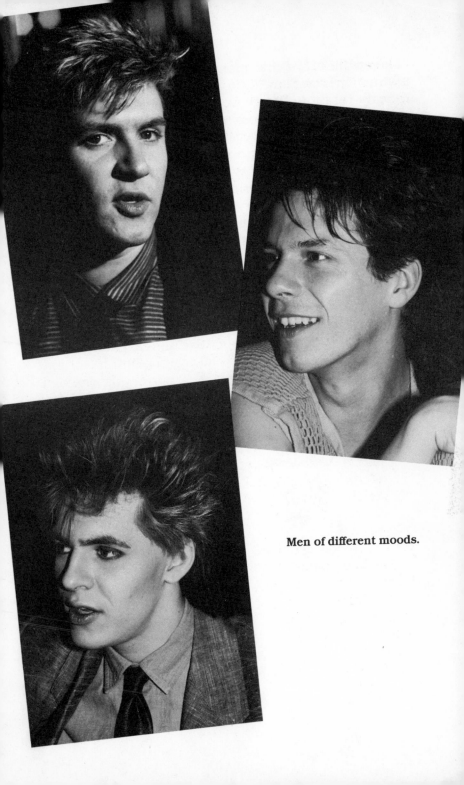

Men of different moods.

Meanwhile, MTV and many video-music shows were playing "Girls on Film," "Rio," and "Hungry like the Wolf" in heavy rotation. People were beginning to notice how interesting the videos looked, as well as how attractive the band was.

By December, this winning combination had worked out in exactly the right way. While the band was touring Europe and playing a series of sold-out concerts in the United Kingdom, "Hungry Like The Wolf" was climbing up the American charts, finally landing at No. 3.

"It was amazing," smiles Simon, "like the biggest birthday present I ever had!"

On December 31, 1982, Duran Duran headlined MTV's live stereo simulcast from the Savoy in New York City. It is estimated that approximately eight million viewers tuned in for the band's sixty-minute set.

This got the year off to a roaring start, and 1983 would certainly be a very special year for Duran Duran.

SEVEN AND THE RAGGED TIGER: The Third Album

Nineteen eighty-three was to be the year Duran Duran conquered the world. That New Year's Eve show, which brought the entire audience (in the club and at home) to its feet cheering, was just the beginning.

With "Hungry like the Wolf" and then "Rio" sitting comfortably at the top of the American charts, Duran Duran went back into the studio and came up with "Is There Something I Should Know?"

But America was still devouring the *Rio* album and the faces that went with it. And when Duran Duran returned here in March, the fans were ready.

When Nick, Simon, Andy, Roger, and John stepped off the plane at Kennedy Airport, a scene reminiscent of the Beatles' first arrival in the States awaited them: Hundreds of screaming, fainting girls crowded around them just to get a glimpse of the guys or grab a fistful of hair.

Cornered a few days later, Nick laughed off the excitement. "The only thing that does irritate me is when people rip buttons and things off clothes. That sometimes gets irritating, but it doesn't happen very often, and when it does, the kids don't really mean any harm. It's just that they get really excited, and it's just something you have to accept."

More of America's first taste of "Durandemonium" awaited the band members when they made a personal

appearance at a video store in Times Square. They had gone there to promote their new video album, which featured eleven previously-released clips, but no one could have predicted that 5000 fans would show up!

By the time "Is There Something I Should Know?" was released in the U.S. (it was added to the first album,

John and Andy join up in rehearsal with Chic's Nile Rodgers. Nile produced David Bowie's last album and is one of John's idols.

which was re-released and zoomed to the top of charts), the members of Duran Duran were in the south of France, writing songs for their next album.

The next stop was Montserrat, a beautiful island in the Caribbean, where they recorded the LP which they had decided to call *Seven and the Ragged Tiger*. (Other artists who have used the same secluded recording facilities include Stevie Wonder, Paul McCartney, Elton John, and the Police.)

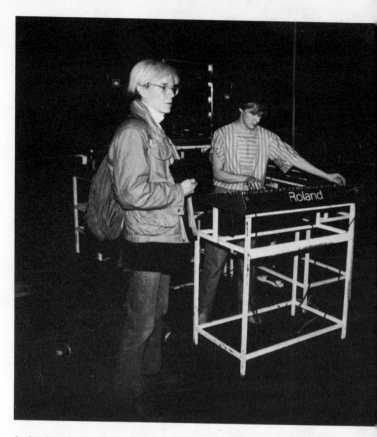

Why did they choose that location? "The main reason," says Simon, "was to get away from all the people who would be popping into the studio if we'd done it in England."

Nonetheless, they weren't completely alone. Andy's wife, Tracey, had come along, and Simon's fiancée, Claire Stansfield, and Nick's girlfriend, Julie Anne Friedman, flew in on weekends. Recording, of course, was the major activity, but the guys had fun swimming, surfing, racing minibikes, and playing table tennis and pool.

July brought them back to England to play for charity before Prince Charles and Princess Diana. The Princess turned out to be quite a fan and said sympathetically to

Famous artist Andy Warhol visited with the band at a New York rehearsal.

Simon, "Have you all been practicing furiously? You must be exhausted. I don't envy you!"

A few days later, the band played a benefit for MEN-CAP, a charitable organization, at Villa Park, a sports stadium in Birmingham. Then it was back to work on the album, this time to mix it in Sydney, Australia.

"We're just like gypsies at the moment," Andy said at the time. "We decided this year, especially as we're working so much, not to live anywhere. It just seems pointless living anywhere because, if you do, you're tied to its laws and boundaries. I think it's good to be out and away, to see other things."

And see other things they certainly did. They spent quite a long time in Sydney. It was rumored that they spent a lot of money as well. Their accommodations reportedly cost over $50,000, the album cover about the same amount, and the "Union of the Snake" video, shot on film, supposedly set them back $100,000, not to mention the cost of hundreds of hours of recording studio time.

But all of it was money well spent, and by the time *Seven and the Ragged Tiger* was released in November, the group was very pleased with what had been accomplished.

Simon explains the album's title: "It's an adventure story about a little commando team. The 'seven' is for us—the five band members and the two managers—and the 'ragged tiger' is success. Seven people running after success. It's ambition. That's what it's about."

Andy speaks for the group in saying, "This is probably the album we wanted to make first time around, but it takes a few to get it right."

Andy really concentrates on his solos.

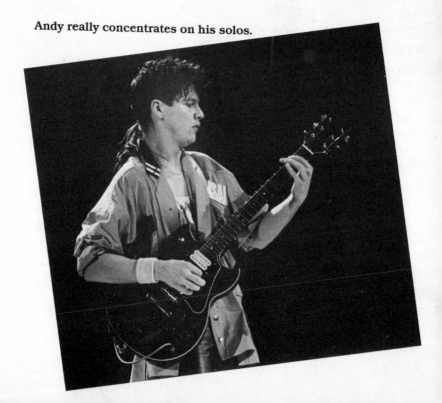

NEW MOON ON MONDAY:
The Future

In November 1983, Duran Duran began its 1983–1984 world tour in Australia. Then came stops in Europe and an English tour, which wound up with five spectacular shows at the huge Wembley Arena.

The U.S. was next. Duran Duran began its tour February 7, 1984, in Los Angeles and wound it up in April. Along the way they stopped to pick up two well-deserved Grammys—one for their video album which contained their first eleven videos, and one for their "Hungry like the Wolf" clip, thus beating out superstar Michael Jackson in that category.

Every date sold out within hours after ticket sales were announced, and for good reason: Even for Duran Duran, the shows were remarkable. Six Roman columns, reminiscent of those in the photo on the *Seven and the Ragged Tiger* cover, lined the back of the stage. What seemed like thousands of lights shone brightly upon the expressive faces of the band. A percussionist, a sax player, and two backup singers joined the on-stage contingent, and the show, which featured all the band's hits, went on spectacularly for nearly two hours.

John now recalls planning for this day. "When we were starting," he says, "Nick and I actually envisaged

"We're *not* the Beatles!" the guys insist at a recent press conference.

what stage we should be at each year, worldwide, and we've surpassed what I wanted!

"It wasn't just sitting and dreaming," he insists. "It was, like, 'Hammersmith by '82, Wembley by '83, Madison Square Garden by '84'—it really was as cut and dried as that. We were so confident in the music and in what we felt we could do, and it was just a matter of how long it was going to take us to get there."

So what's next for a band that's achieved everything it wanted? Let Roger, the quiet one, answer that. "We'll always keep going for new heights," he says. "But maintaining it is probably harder than actually getting there!"

Is it? Nick sums it all up with a flash of that famous Duran Duran grin. "There's nothing else I'd rather be doing at the moment!" he says, and you know there's nothing else you'd rather hear.

Nick and Simon have gotten so good at autographing that they can sign hundreds of photos in an hour. Five thousand fans turned out for this appearance at a New York store.

HOW TO GET IN TOUCH WITH DURAN DURAN

The best way to get in touch with Duran Duran is to write in care of the band's management company. The address is:

Duran Duran
c/o Tritec Ltd.
273 Broad Street
Birmingham, England B1 D2S

Remember that air mail postage to England is 40 cents per half-ounce. Be sure to make your envelope Air Mail. You can also reach Duran Duran's Official Fan Club at this address and get information on how to join.

It is not a good idea to try to call the members of the band, either when they are at home or while they are on tour. They simply do not have time to speak with every fan, although they wish they did. You will only succeed in annoying the guys and their staff, frustrating yourself, and running up your phone bill to ridiculous heights.

You can also write to Duran Duran in care of the record company. The band members will appreciate this because they like the executives there to know how much support they get from their fans, and the mail does get forwarded. The address is:

Duran Duran
c/o Capitol Records
1370 Avenue of the Americas
New York, New York 10019

DISCOGRAPHY

Title   *Release Date*

ALBUMS
Duran Duran (no longer in print)   June 1981
Rio   May 1982
Duran Duran (with "Is There Something I Should Know?"
    added)   April 1983
Seven and the Ragged Tiger   November 1983

MINI-ALBUMS
Carnival (no longer in print)   September 1982

SINGLES
"Planet Earth"/"To The Shore"   June 1981
"Girls on Film"/"Faster than Light"   September 1981
"Hungry like the Wolf"/"Careless Memories"   June 1982
"Rio"/"Hold Back the Rain"   October 1982
"Hungry like the Wolf (Remix)"/"Hungry like the Wolf
    (Night Version)"   December 1982
"Rio (Remix)"/"Hold Back The Rain"   March 1983
"Is There Something I Should Know?"/"Careless
    Memories"   May 1983
"Union of the Snake"/"Secret Oktober"   October 1983

12-INCH SINGLES
"Is There Something I Should Know? (Monster Mix)"/"Faith in This
    Color"   June 1983
"Union of the Snake (Monkey Mix)"/"Union of the Snake (Single
    Version)," "Secret Oktober" October 1983

All released in the U.S. on Capitol Records, except * released on
    Harvest Records.

VIDEOGRAPHY

Duran Duran's first eleven videos are included in the band's video album, which was released in March 1983 by Thorn–EMI Video. They won a Grammy for this.
"Planet Earth"
"Careless Memories"
"Girls On Film"
"My Own Way"
"Hungry Like The Wolf"
"Save A Prayer"
"Rio"
"Lonely In Your Nightmare"
"Night Boat"
"The Chauffeur"
"Is There Something I Should Know?"

Two Video 45's have been released by Sony:
"Hungry Like The Wolf" (Grammy winner)
"Girls On Film"

To date, two promo clips have been released by Capitol for the Seven and the Ragged Tiger *album:*
"Union of the Snake"
"New Moon on Monday"

ABOUT THE AUTHOR

Susan Martin is a writer who lives in New York. She has 5000 books, 6000 records, and not enough room in her apartment.